D0174753

A FAR ROCKAWAY
OF THE HEART

LAWRENCE
FERLINGHETTI

A FAR ROCKAWAY
OF THE HEART

A NEW DIRECTIONS BOOK

Book design by Sylvia Frezzolini Severance
Manufactured in the United States Of America
New Directions Books are printed on acid-free paper.
First published clothbound by New Directions in 1997
Published simultaneously in Canada by Penguin Books Canada Limited.

Library of Congress Cataloging-in-Publication Data
Ferlinghetti, Lawrence.
    A far rockaway of the heart / Lawrence Ferlinghetti.
      p. cm.
    Includes index.
    ISBN 0-8112-1347-1 (clothbound)
    I. Title.
PS3511.E557F37 1997   96–52782
811'.54—dc21   CIP

New Directions Books are published for James Laughlin
by New Directions Publishing Corporation
80 Eighth Avenue, New York 10011

for

Nancy J. Peters

and for

Allen

if he wants it

A FAR ROCKAWAY
OF THE HEART

1

Everything changes and nothing changes
Centuries end
         and all goes on
               as if nothing ever ends
As clouds still stop in mid-flight
         like dirigibles caught in cross-winds

And the fever of savage city life
                still grips the streets

But I still hear singing
         still the voices of poets
    mixed with the cry of prostitutes
             in old Mannahatta
       or Baudelaire's Paris
     birdcalls echoing
         down the alleys of history
             now renamed
And now it's the nineteen hundreds
       and the Market has crashed again
   And my father drifts by in his fedora
        his eyes on the sidewalk
           a single Italian lira
              and an Indian-head penny
                 in his pocket
     Bootleggers and hearses pass
            in slow motion
  A church tolls its iron bell
       mixed with the sound of car alarms
            in the year two thousand

As new suits hurry to work
                    in swaying skyscrapers
        as newsboys still cry out
                    announcing the latest lunacy

And laughter arises
                on the distant sea

2

Driving a cardboard automobile without a license
                at the turn of the century
        my father ran into my mother
                        on a fun-ride at Coney Island
           having spied each other eating
                  in a French boardinghouse nearby
And having decided right there and then
                    that she was for him entirely
      he followed her into
               the playland of that evening
       where the headlong meeting
                  of their ephemeral flesh on wheels
          hurtled them forever together

And I now in the back seat
                of their eternity
                    reaching out to embrace them

3

A native-born New Yorker
  I was from the Lower Inside
  a part of town much favored by
   addicts of the subjective
          (a subversive group always being investigated)
    as well as buddhists
     and their lower chakras
      and others seeking salvations
       from various realities
             virtual or actual
And losing track
     of where I was coming from
        with the amnesia of an immigrant
   I traveled over
      the extrovert face
         of America
But no matter where I wandered
           off the chart
I still would love to find again
        that lost locality
Where I might catch once more
      a Sunday subway for
          some Far Rockaway of the heart

4

The present is a chance event
    that stretches on and on
                into the future
And becomes it

The present is a piece of time
             a hollow arrow flying both ways
                    through the universe
       an endless happening
           with some mute rhyme or reason
    a postmodern happenstance
              performed by Joseph Beuys
   or some joker in a swallowtail coat
              and a false mustache
   or the Pope
      or some greater Happener

And flesh be grass
        that bends and dies
             in every season
Even as at this instant
        a man in striped pajamas
      comes out on
         an uptown balcony
     and drops his house key
        to an eternal woman on the sidewalk
    but the shining key misses
        her outstretched hand
   and falls through a sewer grating
in the City of New York
       and disappears forever
          into the greater mystery

5

Where is that little fish
        I caught and left on the line
            still swimming in the still water
      under that little bridge
               by Bronx River Parkway
        when I was a boy of nine
                  meaning to return?

Swept away!

And I with it

In flood of time

6

At Ellis Island I saw her

Hair of seaweed
                    against the sun silhouetted
        not an idol in an idyll
                            but a black-and-white photo
            of an Irish Anna Livia
                                descending a gangplank
            her hair falling down
                        around a face still drawn
                                        with hunger
            in the great potato famine of 1848

And whose mother
            did she then become
                        in the wide womb of America?

7

By Brooklyn Bridge
  an elephant stands under the Elevated
    in Eric Drooker's painting
      in *Nation* magazine
        in its issue on
          The Corporatization of the World
In the jungle closing 'round it
  a puma waits with shining eyes
    as a train slides into view
      on its Elevated track
              between empty tenements
                carrying no passengers
                        toward the trumpeting elephant
              who stands below with trunk upraised
                and tusks turned toward the train
                and seems not about to
                              turn and run again
As a naked nymph plays a saxophone upraised
    as exotic birds flit about
      and huge jungle vines
              twine about
                          the Elevated's swaying stanchions
As the sun turns tropic
              over green mansions

8

In that hinternation
that stretches Westward from Manhattan
Autumn finds the natives restless

And we pan down
skimming the landscape
as in a low-flying plane
with camera-eye zooming in

Across the iron cities
cement plains and silted rivers

Across Appalachia

Across Ohio
(first Western frontier)
And down into it

Down into middle America
hinter America
by Great Lakes yearning
by Firelands burning
in Indian Autumn
Redbrick mansions moldering
among the wooded streets
of a hundred winded towns
Under the huge sugar maples
down the canyons of dying leaves
each a hand letting go

Silos in Shiloh Ohio
Among the rust-colored trees
Holsteins by brown cornfields
(stripped in autumn harvest)

Groundswells of land
in Amish country
among the limping horse buggies
and Haunted Hayrides
in pumpkin time
And out in Indian country
'The White Man came
and taught us how
to drink black water
in the morning'
And now his car culture barrels through
Torn teepees bulldozed out
A totem or two tilted up

And in Gambier gardens
the bone-dry branches
of the famous Upsidedown Tree
rattle in the wind

As Thomas Alva Edison
born in Milan Ohio
first sees the light in New Jersey
And bosom buddy Henry Ford
moves the lightbulb's birthplace
lock stock & socket
from Menlo Park to Michigan
And drives off in a dense cloud
of unknowing
into a dubious immortality
having sown the iron seeds
of Autogeddon

9

'History is made
   of the lies of the victors'
      but you would never dream it
         from the covers of the textbooks
            nor from the way the victors are portrayed
               as super-benevolent altruists
                  and lovers of the poor and downtrodden
               who never had a chance to
                    rise up and write their own dubious stories
                    in the mystery we call history
                      (a river blurred with tears
                    or a running sea
                      whose fish change color
                        when cast upon the beach)
And the feelthy rich
   get filthier or richer or whatever
    because money really doesn't 'trickle down'
    but rises like anything hot
And they keep getting more medals
   for bad behavior and for agreeing that Yes
   Justice has been done and
      the stock market is open to everyone Long live usura
      and the jury system is the best ever for
         preserving the status quota
And in fact why not have historians who
         leave blanks in their writings
         to be filled in variously
            depending on who's in power
               and the computer makes changes easy
And anyway history isn't really history
until it's rewritten
or at least until
it repeats itself
And a lot of genocides and massacres

maybe never really happened
so the record should be corrected
like the Holocaust or the rape of Cuba and Nicaragua
    or Cambodia or Timor or you name it
Even though even God can't change
a historical fact
something that's actually happened
like a rape or a kiss
But all those natives
  in all those Third and Fourth World ghettos
  really always wanted to be conquered by
    Cortez the prophesied fair-haired god
      or by Columbus the great white hope
        of Spain and/or Italy
              and stolen continents weren't really stolen
                but were glorious Christian conquests that
                  saved those heathens from themselves
                    Onward Christian Soldiers
And on and on into the sunset
  go the histories about how
    God was always on our side anyway
      and who is more fit to write the story than
        the victors themselves who are the fittest
          having survived and arrived at the summit
            of humanity's blind history
                where the prizes are awarded to the fittest
And anyway everyone except Plato knows that
        Truth Beauty Goodness are all relative
          especially Truth as she is extolled
            in the history books Amen *oh brother*
            can you spare a dime?

10

'Only connect!'
> cried Columbus
>> staring through his telescope
And he scoped it out all right
> the 'new world' as he saw it
And he saw it plain
> made of gold
>> bullion and bloody Marys
And the natives 'like children'
> brought him treasures they had hoarded
>> for the next Coming
>>> of Blondie
> (described in their *fumetti*
>> their tragic comic strips)
And Johan Padan
> topside sailor
>> Genovese *giovane*
>>> illiterate *marinero*
> crossed himself and
> dropped his pantaloons
>> when he gazed upon pure flesh of Indy
>>> for the first time
> his old time religion
>> never having prepared him
>>> for naked animal anima
>>>> with no sense of sin

As nude virgins and shamen
> fell before the blunderbuss
>> *cavallos* crashing up the beaches
>>> of Carib paradisos
> the gold gleaming heavy
>> in the blood-red sands

[13]

And the earth shook with it
        And the earth ran with it
            And fell into the canyons
                                of Wall Street Mainstreet USA

11

I would not make a pact with you

old E.P.

old master poet

caro maestro   *il miglior fabbro*

who 'gathered from the air a live tradition'

Expatriate Ezra

Confused Confucian

The Rip van Winkle of American poetry

I loved you long enough
And then unloved you long enough

For it was you who broke the new wood
        the beautiful masks of your *Personae*
      and lovely 'Audiart Audiart
        Where thy bodice laces start'
        and the glorious grandeur
      of your early *Cantos*
    and the caged cantos in Pisa
      rising still to beauty

But then you began the broken sentences
Fit to print on marble
History's ruined echoings
A sounding palimpsest
summarizing the past by theft and allusion
(a fly's buzz carrying news)

[15]

reckoning our destinies
Polyphonic poet-oracle
mouthing Dante and Confucius
Kuan Yin and Kublai Kahn
Jefferson and John Adams
and General Washington
(father of our effrontery)
At worst an old man's mumbled jumble
of erudicities and profundities
by turns noble and incoherent
Scatter of rain on a mansard roof
mixed with antique gossip
ancient Tuscan account books
and yesterday's conversations
A garrulous gabble of
crackerbarrel colloquial
cobbled into the typography of poetry
in *canti* that couldn't possibly be sung

(But, as you let slip once
in a first draft of the first Canto
'the modern world
needs such a rag-bag
to stuff its thoughts in')

Whereas jaunty Jimmy Joyce—he also polyphonic—
in nearby triste Trieste
had already gone further in forging
'the uncreated conscience' of his race
with his blooming voice
beside the chittering waters of
withering waters of
the talking streams of consciousness
i fiumi della nostra vita

And it was you then
who stoked the wood

into the fascist flame
in the blind world's fire
Old radio-fascist Rip
'Lord Ga Ga' (as the good doctor called you)
Furbo Musso-phile
who gave the fascist salute to friends
mouthing off on Radio Roma
and in vain Venezia
(like D'Annunzio courting Il Duce
before *fascismo* became *fascista*)
So they took you in
the conquerors in khaki
The *americani* took you in
as a traitor or a space-case
And threw you in that cage in Pisa
And took your rage back to America

And you then strolling
in Saint Elizabeth's mental gardens
(sad the long waste years
of blasted genius!)
Until at last released—
Old Rip himself
sprung from the Catskills of his own deep slumber
(having not read or rolled the psychedelic papers
of the new consciousness)
Then split straightaway back to the Old World
the crenelated camembert of Olde Europa

And there in your Venetian dotage
heated up the old pottage
and mumbled a form of repentance
that Jews were your
'stupid suburban prejudice'
but stopped short there
baffled into silence!

[17]

           your *lume* truly *spento*

A *blown husk that was finished*
                                    but the light sang eternal

And the enormous dream
still in your eyes
having beaten out your exile

#12

And Pablo Neruda
        that Chilean omnivore of poetry
      who wanted to
           put everything in
             and take nothing out
                (of his *Canto General*)
   said to me in Havana Libre Hilton 1959
                'I love your wide open poetry'
     by which he meant a certain kind of
        poesía norteamericana
             and its rebel band who
          rose over the rooftops of
               tenement boneyards
            intent on making out
And made out of madness
        a hundred years of beatitude

'So boring I'm snoring'
          cried Joe Public
        before *they* came along
        and busted out the sides
             of *Poetry* Chicago
       and various New Yorkerish
             poetasters
          out of their Westchester cradles
                  endlessly rocking
            on the Times Square Shuttle
        between the *Times Book Review*
               and the Algonquin
      while lady critics and gent professors
            moaned about poetic pederasts
                  at Columbia

They cruised Times Square and America
                    and cruised into history
                    'waving genitals and manuscripts'
And tuned their holy unholy voices
                    to a wide open society
                              that didn't yet exist
And so jump-started
                    the stalled merry-go-round
                                        of American ecstasy
                              left along East River's
                                        echoing shores
                    after Old Walt stepped off
                                        Brooklyn Ferry
                                        into the heart of America

#13

Whereas Einstein was not the James Joyce of scientists and James Joyce was not the Einstein of novelists who no one could go beyond because beyond was a space where all is curved and comes around again to its beginning in a relative sort of way and after all isn't that what a river does always turning back upon itself like a serpent eating its tail which is life itself and everyone's life like a rushing stream down a mountain into the greatest river and the river always coming back to itself after it flows to the ocean and returns in clouds and rain and sunsets although today sunsets are dying the rivers dying and how much longer will the river be returning and returning as if a river really ever could come home again with its voyagers and that far wanderer James Joyce always leaning back to listen to old River Liffey telling him the great tale always whispering to him that wake of words for all of us to wail upon along a riverrun homing in the gloaming

14

The defeated Romanticism
   of T. S. Eliot
         and his pathetic phallusies
                   haunted my schooldays
He would not go away
His spent phrases
     dripped in my inner ear
             whenever a poet was near
Everyone echoed him
        even Anglican preachers
A defrocked Prufrock
  and his exhausted libido
     stalked my boys' school hallways
        hand in hand with
           Mister Quichotte
            the young English tutor
             (He wore his trousers rolled)
Only old Graves
   in First Year Latin
      would not bow down
         sticking to his Juvenal
           and the Bucolics
We were sure at night he tippled
        with Dionysus
  And flung off his Harris tweed and
        mounted the lovely housemaid
             in Honors Cottage
     And heard the mermaids singing
          each to each
        And heard them singing to himself
And off and on made faces at
      a copy of *The Waste Land*
         on a very high shelf

15

And Samuel Beckett's house of cards
   made of silence
       of the pure speech of silence
     the silence between our words
         or others' words and ours
  or the speech we all speak
       upon dying
And Beckett with his silences
   even when young & Irish
     began making his way underground
          toward the total silence of death
It was as if his whole life
     were an end-game
        headed underground
And with Nagg and Nell and Hamm and Clove
       he sank deeper and deeper
And with Krapp he made his Last Tape
       on the way down
And Murphy became Molloy
    and Molloy became Malone
      And Malone died talking
     but his brain continued turning over
         underground
And still much later could be heard
    mutterings
     moanings
      disjointed curses
       baby mouthings
        last gasps
  the last gasps of
    his muted consciousness
     that in spite of all that fall
      fain would not leave us

16

So that
    the God whom humans had decided
      is Consciousness itself
       whose center is the self
        and its circumference
            everywhere
  looked down from the outskirts
    of His empire of the conscious
      in the far suburbs of His kingdom
  where He had set up
    a temporary headquarters
    a sort of summer pavilion
    or rather a winter palace
  since it was quite cold
    way out there in space & time
      and much warmer
      down in the heart & mind of things

And He looked down from His throne
  which was of the portable variety
    sort of like a Port-O-Let
    with handles fore-and-aft
    so that He could be carried
      anywhere as needed
    without dismounting
  because He was always having to move
      on the run
      depending upon
    where His Beings
    human and inhuman
      had shifted their consciousness
    which was constantly expanding
      by natural or non-natural means

So that
       He looked down from His high throne
           and saw light upon the face of the earth
                    and saw that it was good
And He said to Himself looking down
              'It's a good deal!
                    Life is a good deal!'
     although even as He spake it
           He could hear a devilish voice
             behind him whispering
                    'Life sucks'
    which was very discouraging to God
      who would go into these
               deep glooms
   (and some suspected
           he was a manic depressive)
But He
   would always manage to
          climb up and out
  where He could see
        the light on earth again
So that He looked down again
     just this past winter and
         decide to take a New Year's inventory
    and took out his portable Mac
           and started to write down everything
      such as:

One Dutch ship sighting Sandy Hook New Jersey
     and mistaking it for
          the Hook of Holland
One very beautiful woman
     weeping in a restaurant
        her hand held
         by a black lover
One red lobster on a leash
     strolling down a Paris boulevard

One very small dog peeing
     on a very large tree
       in which two birds are
          trying to sing
One roar of an MGM lion
         on a silver screen
One fine day under the Linden trees
        in Boston Common
One ice cream cone about to be licked
         by a boy in short pants
One enlightened politician
        behind bars
One Zapatista
And one fine anarchist picnic
And one monkey playing a masterpiece
            on a computer
One merry-go-round on a deserted playground
   with wooden horses all galloping
     in the same direction
One spent serpent eating its own tail
One cool evening in autumn capitols
        their avenues of leaves ablaze
One Prague symphony written on
        the walls of Auschwitz
And a stone a leaf an unfound door
And a cow a clod a far figure
   by a railroad crossing at dusk
     to flash upon a Pullman window
        and be gone
And the great cracked bell of St. Sulpice
        shaking the dusk of Paris
And Mother in a manger
  because no room at an inn
And a kid called Jesus
     posing as a Christchild

And a flight of blackbirds
    over the Appian Way
        where legions in battle dress
            are once again marching
And one hot soccer star
        wearing a Forza Italia armband
And six hundred and forty-three delegates
        to an over-population conference
            walking out on the Pope
                who refuses to wear a condom
And one egg
        rolling under a pushcart
           pursued by three billion people
And one moment of silence
And one moment of epiphany
One moment of ecstasy
One moment of madness
And one moment of silence

And still looking down at everything
           God spake in tongues and said:
    'Ah yes
        and these are all thoughts I acted out
            but they were only tryouts for
                the real thing'
And hence He started to sing
      in his *vox populi*
          a whole new opera
    (all of which turned out to be
          the libretto for
             our twenty-first century)
     with a singing part for every heart
     and even a part
         for the very heart
           of our ungodly
             unconscious

17

Do dreams rescue your ego
        as an ocean saves a sinking ship?
Things you cannot deal with
      in waking life
        like an iceberg off the bow
          are transformed in dreams
            to something you
              can throw a lifeline to
                or recognize as some pale idol
                or familiar monster
                  whom you have already
                    learned to deal with
     like some old friend or lover
      still coming around
        for free kisses
        or other doubtful blisses

So that you wake with some elation
        and instead of the torments of
                  the great hereunder
        you hear again the ego's
            erotic thunder

And await the lightning's
        next illumination

#18

Narcissus always carried
        a small hand mirror
                just in case there was no water
    to see the self in
           like most of the rest of humanity
              carrying their little vanities
And the child
    for the first time seeing
             a shell of the self
             (and shocked by the sight of it)
Spends the rest of life enslaved
    to this so-true-and-false
              mirror image
  and only now and then seeing
          over a shoulder
            the world beyond the mirror
    and never reflecting
       that life itself
          be only a samsara illusion
    in the hand-held mirror of
        some Higher Narcissus
      leaning over our
        little quivering pool
  In which might still be reflected
              a totally Ideal Being

#19

So rent a museum
                and see yourself in mirrors—
In every room an exposition
                 of a different phase in your life
with all your figures and faces
        and pictures of all the people who
                    passed through you
    and all the scenes
              you passed through
     all the landscapes of living
              and longing and desiring
               and spending and getting
               and doing and dying
            and sighing and laughing and crying
                (what antic gesturing!)
And walking through the house of yourself
        you climb again to all
              the rooms of yourself
    full of the other lives & selves
            who passed through them
Rooms rooms rooms
     piled up haphazard
         in the architecture of time
And all the bodies clinging to each other
     or rushing to windows
      to break out of the room
         which they boxed themselves into
All the people of your life
      in one house in the night
            all lights lit
       like a cruise ship at sea

And you run up and down
                    knocking on all the doors
        through which you hear
                       all the once-familiar voices
                            laughing or sobbing or singing
And you run to the roof
        and look up to the mute night sky
            And in the wheeling template of stars
                see the faces the figures
                    of the lovely lovers who
                        had once made time stand still
            now all fixed
                        in their constellated relations
                    motionless in time

So that
        some day
            as time bends around
                            to its beginning again
                you find them all again
                            and yourself

20

When the senses awake before the mind
      And a bird sings
           in a far tree
   It is not the mind that hears it
         but an ear of what we call the soul
    which may exist
        only if we think it

And love what is love
   and heart what is heart
     if we don't think they exist
The winged petal fallen away
             will not tell us
   though it be shaped like a heart
         upsidedown and brittle as a leaf
And my book is full
       of leaves and petals picked
          before they fell apart
And they are veined and winded
       like the heart

21

O
heart
involuntary muscle

O
heart
mute lover
without a tongue
of your own

I would speak for you
whenever you
(seeing a certain someone)
feel love

22

In lock of love

lacklove forgotten

lovers lie down

and unlock the dove

of passion

each in his

or her own fashion

And all is anew

in lock of love

begotten

23

The lovers under the portico

in the first Spring rain

Held each other by the heart

Like wet green leaves

clinging together

that even in the driest weather

Would not fall apart

24

She didn't believe
                in ecstasy
She didn't believe
                in wild flights
    that would later
                    fall to the ground
                        (without parachutes)
Yet was still a romantic
                    in her own ways
        having spent her salad days
            loving a painter who flew
                    where she never cared to
                                    dare to

25

An obscure composer
                    she was
    but not so obscure as
                    to compose
                                obscure musicks
She composed people instead
                        into amorous clusters
        at her summer musters
                at the old homestead
So that they fell naturally
                    into each other's armatures
And no harm if yours
        was among the few
            that fell further into
                            the too deep grass
                                where swain might meet swain
            or lad meet lad
                    or lad meet lass
And many were the swain songs
        as swan met swan
                        and ass ass

#26

He made the usual fool of himself
        with the women that night
                (as if there were still roses left
                        in the garden of love)
    throwing off his striped pajamas at the
                      wrong moment
           and generally putting
              the wrong emphasis
                    on the wrong words
   which left him much exposed
        to the dumb winds of chance
        which in his case usually blew
        through his pants
A regular walking calamity he was
  and certainly no match
    for any carnivorous kid
     or that omnivorous
           DeKooning woman with the scythe
                who was very much into
                   eating him alive
    And she did she did

#27

It's a woman's world
    despite what they say
And I not one of them
    letting my male chauvinism
              hang right out
                          once in a while on purpose
Like barking up a tree
        in which a siren cat
           has taken refuge
              from a dog's world
      stretched out up there
                hidden among the leaves
          languourous
              enigmatic
        long-haired and
             sinuous as a lynx

  And totally in control of the situation

#28

I heard a woman making love today
                              to some beast
Through the wall I heard her voice cry out
                                        in ecstasy
                              or pain or joy
                                    at least
And it was too late
                to do anything about it
                                    except go with it
                                                or doubt it
Instead I ran through the streets
                              wearing a mask
                                    and singing mad songs
Then fell into a zoo
      tore off my clothes
            and sprang in among the animals
                              those adepts at loneliness
And lay down with them
                        in that unpeaceable kingdom
And fell asleep like a gypsy
                        dreaming of a lioness lover

#29

And love be written on running water
                              not on the surface
                                of calm lakes

And a hummingbird writes it
                              dancing above the stream
     and disappears
                    leaving only
                            the sound of its wings
While the moving water
                    sings through the sluices
                                    of everyday life

30

The lover leaves the house of her lover

The flower of her face

        the petals of her lips

                wound the sleeping street

And she disappears down it

        as down a funnel

            through which all life has poured

#31

She came in out of the night
   Stood in the doorway wavering
             like a leaf blown
                    against a window
And fluttered past
         in the first wind

    a wine-glass leaf
          a leaf out of autumn

And fluttered away
         And wandered away

Adrift in the maze
        of her own wild life . . .

3 2

Think back through the long years

Laughter in the eucalyptus forest

And the sighs no one hears

The green lush trees still there

And the long leaves like hair

                      still streaming in the wind

And the sea's voice far off

            still sounding

              upon the breakers pounding

The earth still breathing there

Though the heart be swept bare

33

How the light
        lay on the leaves
How the light
        glinted through them

How the leaves themselves
            were light
How all creatures there
        were light
            were made of light
      the warp of light
           upon them

In the dawn of the world that year

And they
      pulsed with it
          with light of earth
    as if they
          always would be
              full of light
              made of light

Shimmering

Among the sere and yellow leaves

In the autumn of that year

#34

Light knows rain
                and how to use it
    But the rain
             knows not light
      until light hits it
                  and transforms it
Just as man sleeping
              knows not light
   but is transformed in waking
                 as light falls on eyelids
     trembling with dawn

And man gets up
           and puts his lenses on

35

Pure white in first light

Pure as some angel
        the canvas stood
                before the young painter

It pulsed in waves of light

It had its own radiance

He could only sully it
        bully it
            with his too-harsh brush
      violate it
        with his too-phallic palette knife

He wished for a brush of fine white feathers
      (the Swan with Leda)

And he stood back

And he laid the canvas down

And lay down with it alone

And long he lay with that virgin
        lusting for a purity his own

36

Day after day returning
                    to paint the same picture over & over
        the monster canvas implacable
                        containing every place & race
        and absorbing every strike & blow
                    like some stone-faced boxer
                            weaving & deceiving
                    fading in & out

It is a fight to the last clout

        to find the eye of the beast unblinking
                                inscrutable
            And *nail* it
                    And lay out its carapace

And with the open paint can
                        full of unknown alphabets
        pour or paint or print or stamp upon it
                                a final face

37

The party hoppers
                    wolfing down the wine and cheese
        without a glance at what might be
                             considered art
At all those Thursday evening openings
                    in San Francisco galleries
And the critics and the crickets
                and the singles out to score
And the docents of the donor classes
            sheathed in silk & Christian Dior
                    holding long-stemmed glasses

With the tide of tinkled voices rising

And the painter to one side apprising
                the whole uprising
                    as if from a most distant shore
  And saying to himself Is *this*
                what I am painting for?
No wonder then that he
            adrift in this society
  doth drink too much
            and roll upon the floor?

38

A cricket somewhere
                winds his watch

A swatch of sunlight
                washes across the landscape

A Van Gogh crow
             lets out a cry
                        carrying night on its wing
His flying shadow
             haunts the sky

In which I
          dip my paintbrush

39

A blue-bottle fly
                    alighted on my palette
     and started walking around
          my squeezed-out landscape
               the paint laid out in patches
                    of mixed color
                         to match the land before me
I watched in horror as the fly
  walked right into
          the yellow-ochre of
                              that California autumn
It was fate for the fly
               whose feet stuck instantly
                              in the deep color-field
So then he began
                    to flutter his wings
                              so frantically
     but he stuck fast in the golden clay
                    though he tried and tried
                              to fly away
Yet still he dragged himself
                              to the edge of that flat world
And then fell off
                    spinning dizzily
                              like a broken helicopter
And crashed with a terrible cry
                    inaudible to me

40

When the painter Pissarro lay dying
he looked surprised
as if he had not expected to see
so much blue
in the landscape of
his afterlife
And his eyes got wider and bluer
even though his eyes were already all blue
('Old Blue' they called him)
A crooked smile
tangled his beard
and his hand passed over it
wiping out the smile
a trace of which remained
in his surprised eyes
which remained wide open
as life left him
like windows on the endless landscape
inside him
which he had all his life
been painting

41

By the statue of Rodin
                    I sat down and wept
This metal cast from his clay
                  the living clay
                         in his image
                                Come to this!
How could it die
             his genius clay
                     fall into nothingness
     dissolve in earth and sky
                     disappear from us
Seer who saw with his fingers
                    Felt all
                         with his hands
Maestro maker and imaginer
                    realist supreme
     life lover and death defier
                        Eros eternal
          Molding heads
               with one hand
                    out of our dust
        breathing life into it
                    Great clay images
                           of us
        (heroic and pathetic!)
                       breathing life eternal
How then himself
          his own clay body
                  fallen apart
         rotted down
                  to dust
   and resurrected here
              in metal effigy?
                     Ah Rodin—Rodin!

42

In the catalog raisonné
                of Hieronymus Bosch
  the medieval imagination
          struggles up
                  through the dank Dark Ages
               with its hallucinations and live chimeras
               and its horrible fear of Hell
As Bosch himself sloshes through
                 the visionary swamps of his painting
          wielding a wicked paintbrush
          loaded with the first liquid light
          of the first dawn seen
             since the diamond light of Greece
       with which he painted the first crack
       in the sky of the medieval night
        through which then poured
        his fantastic horde of
          heretic erotics
          platonic ecstatics
        pagan ascetics
      anarchist alchemists
    singing sibyls and libertine layabouts
   angels and monks and animals
       doing heavenly things to each other
     in Rube Goldberg chains of being
      in paradisos and purgatorios
      of their own making—
     all 'Brothers & Sisters of the Free Spirit'
    a secret heretic cult
     to which Bosch himself belonged
       and for whom he painted
         his hidden heresies
   (while all the while doing straight jobs
             for the Church)

And the illuminati of
    this counterculture cult
        in secret underground rites
            acting out their reincarnations of love
                in the spaced-out spirit of the Holy Ghost
                    exalted to a state of spiritual perfection
                    and immune from Sin
                        even in flesh on earth
                as if they had found a way
                    back into a permanent Paradise
        where they now lived and loved
                in the purest state of erotic innocence

And that only the beginning
        of the supra-sensual liberation
                        of enslaved true believers
                        enchained for centuries
            with El Bosco and his brush depicting
            a lady serpent in a tree
            offering a new apple to
                a reconstituted Adam & Eve
                    (with Eve taller than Adam)
Only this time around
                they are incorruptible
            having learned from their primeval therapists
            that they didn't *have* to accept
                    the shame of Original Sin
            which their old guilt-driven religion
                        was still laying on them
And Bosch further depicting
            a whole phantasmagoria of pure extasis
                in the first garden of divine delight
                    in which Adam was the original hairy man
                    and Eve as glabrous as light itself
                        on the First Morning redawning
And flesh was grass
                (and living beings all leaves of grass)

in a great 'Hay Wagon' of God's Harvest
and in his 'Millennium'
with its myriad liberated lovers
(woman and man and animal)
And Seven Deadly Sins hung out to dry
with their too lively sons
And a Ship of Fools in flames
beyond which floats a thatched church
with a woman's head for a roof
and a naked maid in its open door
near a prone dreamer
with a lizard for penis
And Death with a spear
behind an uncertain curtain
And a nude nun beating the bare buns
of a bent-over blond
while an avid pig in nun's clothing
embraces a pavid parishioner
And an armored animal with human legs
mounts a man stretched out
on the strings of a harp
as a hidden hand fingers a vulva
and beats the bung of a drum
from which music notes are strung
And a horny unicorn drinks
from a fountain of couth youth
And an Avenging Angel with sword upraised
chases a terrified Adam & Eve
into a dark wood
While multi-cultural couples disport
in heavenly hot springs
with birds and apples on their heads
and bathers on nude beaches by blue lakes
cling together kissing
with mouths missing
but tongues entwined

While out of a deep
                    egg-shaped pond
                         all kinds of retro creatures crawl
                              toward the golden light of day
As a flight of flapping Jurassic monsters
    pours through a futurist sculpture
         mounted on a fertile turtle
Beyond which waits a knight in fish-scale armor

And the scales weighing everything
                              in that Garden of Earthly Delights
                    in which El Bosco saw
                              not the Natural History of Evil
    where all would burn forever for their sins
         as the True Church chose to see it
  but the real world as he saw it
         a derisive allegory
              of libidinous life on present earth
    as if Evil were really nothing but
                              a tragicomic side-effect
         and his paintings actually
              the secret psychedelic posters for
                   the liberated orgies of his time

43

In the Beginning
            wasn't the Word
  since we name an image
                after we see it
As for instance when
           that time
                before the beginning of rhyme
When Adam one morning
             went out wordless
         into the gloaming
                of his early morning Garden
And speechless saw
         for the first time
               the sun rise radiant
                   over the rim of the world
And then burst out
         with an inchoate sound of ecstasy
              a wordless mantra to the sun
And he had no word for it
       until much later he bit
         into the big apple of knowledge
         with its wondrous
                pips of words

44

Reaching into the great abyss
                        of the world's long night
And presuming that in the Beginning
                                was Darkness
                    and Light just the afterglow
                                        of a red shift
The poet
            fathoming the unknown
                        like a deep ocean trawler
        drags for primal images
                    with gillnet wordnets out to catch
                            the last wild *lingua franca*
                                the blind fish of man's fate

45

Oh you gatherer
  of the fine ash of poetry
    ash of the too-white flame
       of poetry

Consider those who have burned before you
      in the so-white fire

Crucible of Keats and Campana
    Bruno and Sappho
        Rimbaud and Poe and Corso
   And Shelley burning on the beach
       at Viarreggio

And now in the night
   in the general conflagration
    the white light
      still consuming us
   small clowns
    with our little tapers
      held to the flame

46

And every poem and every picture
                    a sensation in the eye and heart
Something that jolts you awake
                    from the rapt sleep of living
              in a flash of pure epiphany
                    where all stands still
                                    in a diamond light
        transfixed
                    revealed
                          for what it truly is
                                        in all its mystery
So a bird is an animal
                    flown into a tree
                                    singing inscrutable melodies
As a lover stands transparent
                    screened against the sun
                          smiling darkly in the blinding light

47

In far-out poetry
        the heart bleeds upon the page
                    shamelessly
    as printer's ink bleeds onto
              the fine tooth of paper
As blood in its rage
        beats through the body
               blind in its courses
Leaving its indelible imprints
        those fine tattoos of living
               known as poems

48

O fragile poems
                flowers of night-love
Quivering of guitars
                  by the Guadalquivir
Echoed voices
            on sunlit terraces

White statues on bridgeheads
                     And 'the white arms of roads'
Leap of wild horses
              pawing the earth
Trains in the night
            their haunted whistles hid
                        in book of time
Autumn evenings on Third Avenue
                  the ochre light falling
Dressmakers' dummies undressed
                on tenement fire escapes
Newborn babies thrust
            into baths of tears
Laughter like crystal shattering
                Champagne glasses thrown
                        against fireplaces
Dawn and the exhausted lovers
              still to be sated—

All, all poems in the human dream
              still to be liberated!

49

Never a madman
Yet never far
from ludic laughter
A stand-up tragedian
I'd still absurdly ask the ultimate
of art and poetry
Only the absolute need apply
(ah hypocrite postmodern, pass by!)
Bare beauty
like a rock statue in an ocean
above the waves unbreachable
The Goddess bald
or the Godhead shaven
seen full-on
Let them turn toward us
gesturing
insurgent
And shake the world
shake our senses
sensors and censors
Let the walls of the temple shake
and concrete cities crumble
Let the stars shine through
A hole in heaven
(as through the dome of the Pantheon)
to see the ultimate
white night
the final
antic vision

#50

The mind dances
        when the body lets it

And when the body cannot
        the mind dances within

But sometimes they move together
         and together sway
        and fly together
          and dance and sing

And then it is indeed
        an enchanting thing

51

The dance of the mind
   through Mozart's wind concertos
      with only one part of the flashing brain

            illuminated at any one time
And then at the very ending
         as at the climax of a Living Theatre play

  the whole astounding head
           seen for the first time
   the movements turning together

         as inside a crystal clock
      enmeshed in a great crescendo
           as if all the piercing insights

   of an impassioned lifetime
        now sang together in one great
     lyric breakthrough
         into inner space

52

The leaves danced to Mozart
                    above the world's static

It was an art they could understand

It was as if
          some god were listening
                              through them
        and dancing with them
                        ecstatic

53

Death comes on
> like a Beethoven concerto
> the composer himself on the stand
> both arms extended
> to his own skies
> the deep heaven of his orchestra
> driven to escape that absolute silence
> which he knows will come
> with the last movement

And he raises his shaggy mane
> and shakes his hoary locks

And all falls
> deafening
> upon him
> in the final unheard chord

54

I wring the neck of the swan
    the horn of the old-fashioned
        wind-up phonograph
I wring the neck of nostalgia
    but the throaty voice
        keeps coming out
           eternal
   in that smokey jazz *cave*
      under the Deux Magots
        Saint Germain midnight
And Piaf singing
    in her Parigot argot
        Je ne regrette rien
         Je ne regrrrette rrrrien . . .
The orphan's eyes
    the black short dress
      the huskless voice
        made of smoke and Pernod

The mask of her face
    fallen out of darkness

55

The cat doing kundalini

arches his back and

stretches up

doing the Flight of the Swan

with Leda looking on

56

A very large cat ate a singing bird
And the cat digested the birdsong
and started singing and
then a very large dog came along
and heard the cat singing
and said to himself
If only I could sing like that
And so the dog ate the cat
and the dog started singing
and a ferocious wild lion
who just happened to be in the neighborhood
heard the dog singing like a bird
and said to himself If only I could sing like that
my old lady might let me back into
her nice warm cave
and so the lion ate the singing dog
and sure enough the lion
started singing very sweetly
(if a bit extra loud)
And then a postmodern man came along
and heard the lion singing
where he lay rolling in the grass
and the man said to himself
This is what we have all lost and
if I eat the singing lion perhaps
we can get it all back
including my mind
And so the man ate the lion and then
the man started singing
as if pure lyricism
hadn't been banned
in the postmodern world
And pretty soon all the men & women on earth
started singing together

(if a bit off-key)
and their music reached to the skies
a very fine musick indeed
But then one fine day
the universe swallowed the world whole
and the whole universe
like one sentient being
fell into a new perfect harmony
And it was the true music of the spheres
a visionary music
                    a slow music
  an andante music
                          a singing in the inner ear

57

The Italian-American bimbo from Brooklyn
        assured me we had
                the best seats on the plane
And indeed they were
    except for the First Class passengers
                up front
       who lay back like
            they would get there
                long before us
     or were about to
           fly to heaven
    having been provided with
         tiny little sets of silver wings
            which they waved languidly
     between sips of champagne and caviar
        and all the while smiling sweetly
               at each other
  as if they never had killed
         their first mates
    with daggers in their eyes
       nor had ever said
           a mean word to anyone
     in all their beautiful lives

And all the rest of us
     just sitting there
         row on row as evermore
   with our boxed lunches
  and our bare faces hanging out
     looking just like proles
        in Orwell's woeful *1984*

#58

The plane wings away toward heaven
and an angel's multilingual voice
                        comes over the headphones
                sensual as Sappho
                        (ah why is the erotic
                                so despotic?)
And it's Italian opera all the way
                        across gigantic Atlantic
        with these flying orchestras—
                        How they soar!
        Forty thousand feet is nothing
                        in this stratosphere of
                Verdi   Puccini   Rossini
And it's still unreal
                this winged metal creature hurtling
        through the dark air
                        heir to Icarus
                lighted eyes curtained
                        into the red dawn
                over old Europa
                        which we swoop over now
                like Ruskin's eagle
                        over the Apennines

What white cliffs What grey headlands!

Ah but they are only clouds
                alto cumulus
                        towering up

And there's the sea again
                    Mare mediterraneo
          Old ships still
                         set forth on it
     Columbus
               sets out his signal flags

As we come floating in

59

The vast port sways with creaking cordage
Lost among outcries of evening
and the million eyes of autos
in the resounding city—

Lush Sicilian madonna
                    with lip-hung cigarette
Flesh octopus with raucous laugh
    hangs out a glassless window
             in the dark cave of
                   a Genovese alley
A debased heat flows
from the iron arms of the city
flooding up through flesh
              to the rouged nipples

And myriad men in the eternal night
            with limp cocks and unfed hearts
                  stagger away
                      through the centuries

60

Roma	Rome
La pioggia	Rain
sul Tevere	on the Tiber
Le foglie	Leaves
cadono	fall
come	like
gocce	raindrops
E la notte	And the night
viaggia	voyages
attraverso	through
l'oscurita	the darkness

61

Roma

made of flesh and stone

madness and misery

laughter and forgetting

In the shadow of its night streets

sleeps the old dream:

Light out of night

The sun bursts forth

over the Piazza del Populo

62

"Ooops, Pamplona!" cried the Pope
      Or "Stromboli!"
           depending how volcanic he felt
                    whenever he came
(according to the bird sitting next to Him
at the press banquet)
with all the other hacks gaga
to hear what we were saying
My pencil at the ready
I leaned into her and asked
"So you had the Pope for a boyfriend
before he was Pope?"
She was tiny, with a loony look
She wrote for the Vatican blatt
She had a high voice
sort of peepy and cracked
She had feathers in her bird's-nest hat
"He loved all mankind"
She sang in little bursts
"And womankind!"
"I *adored* him" she whispered
her little mouth half-open
"And whenever he came
he always cried 'Ooops, Pamplona!'
Or 'Oops, Stromboli!'
And we went swimming a lot . . . birthday suits!"
"Birthday suits," I repeated
scribbling like mad
As she fell silent
"Actually,"
she blurted out at last
"He's a secret anarchist"
as she stood up on the table
and flew away
over the rooftops. . . .

63

Rear-guard galleries
in the Via Margutta
Cats sunning themselves
on terracotta rooftops
The sun coming over

And then in the Testaccio
the hunger for life continues
as elsewhere
only fiercer
as wherever there are animals
devouring each other
figuratively or otherwise

And far off
lost in future time
across the river
very distantly
heard and not heard
intermittently
(almost an echo of itself)
an iron bell tolls
in a clay cathedral
ringing out the end
of the Christian era

64

On the stage set
of the Piazza della Rotunda
A couple of thousand citizens
(some still in togas)
strolling about or
sitting at café tables
And an old old flowerseller
passing among the tables
bending over young couples in jeans
as they whisper together
and offering them
her so dry flowers
And they not deigning
to notice the old crone
with her gnarled hands
and her fingers full of
the thin rings of
her former lives
each one of them enough
to enlighten them
as to what love or life might be
And her lips
almost at their ears
in which they hear only
the very distant roaring
of their own futures

65

In the *sala di pranzo*
a swarm of tourists
in their morning feeding frenzy
And then they're all swept away
into one huge tour bus
And one little table left
with one very old French couple
having their croissant breakfasts
si civilisés
and discoursing in their so refined voices
si cultivés
the old *mémère* and the old *père*
his fallen face just like his lady's
And all that's left of his virility
is his deep voice
rumbling up
sounding up from his lower depths
as if beneath the table
Eros still stirred

66

Walking through the University of Bologna
               the oldest university in the world . . .
The usual protests by unusual students
           stoning the administration
            for Giordano Bruno
             or Garibaldi
              or Pasolini
                or La Lotta Continua
And the usual statues under the arcades
                  or under the trees
           Great yellow leaves
               falling on them
And the gardens full of
     stone philosophers
       oblivious
         above it all
            having survived their own
                dying fall
As I release a singing bird
from under my hat
And join the nearest demonstration
against virtual reality
led by Umberto Eco I suppose
or a wit that looks like him
         waving a rose

67

I saw great Neptune
                    in a piazza fountain in Bologna
        with his tall trident
                        standing over four fat stone women
                                        squeezing their own breasts
            and water spouting out of them
                        into the fountain's stone pool
Only it was only
                    a huge billboard photo
                                    set up where the women
                                    were supposed to be
            since they were really lying down
                                        inside a nearby palazzo
                        where they were being restored
                                    as in some classic beauty parlor

And would the greatest beauticians
                                in all the world
            really be able to restore
                                    those acid-eaten breasts
            those globes of the world
                        those ravaged images of
                                        its late fate

68

In the hills above Firenze
                    the fireflies
        in the heart of night
                        in the tall grasses
    by the tall Italian cypresses
            Tiny tiny soft sparklers
                    like the eyes of magic winged faeries
    flitting about
                silent in the soft darkness
  With tiny tissue-paper eyelids
                    they blink mutely
                            on and off
                    off and on
        in the still silence
                    of the country night

And Pasolini was mistaken
There still are fireflies
                    on earth at night
And the world
        not about to end
                    in a dearth of light

69

Kids blowing bubbles
        in front of the pizzeria
High noon *mezzogiorno*
       and the grown-ups oblivious
       of the glorious worlds
           contained in each bubble
    scintillating in sunlight
        blown by the newborn bambino
              (still in his crib)
       and stared at in dumb wonder
                (if not surprise)
    Worlds within worlds aglow
        in each little floating globe
      alight in the sunshine
        and floating away in space
          and soundlessly exploding
             into Nothingness
From whence this
       new kid on the block
          did just arise

70

A mass in progress in the listing church
    of Santa Maria Madre
        in this little lost port
            on the little island of Procida
The Virgin in a glass case
    with a gold crown of stars and
        a gold halo also with stars
           behind the altar high up
      the Virgin carrying
          the dying Christ in her arms
And the priest moans in a high voice
           almost singing
      keening disconsolate
And the bent fishermen with bare heads
    and the fisher wives and widows
        with black handkerchieves on their heads
        all kneeling there
      and actually weeping
    as they stare up at
         the limp Christ
    as if he had only fainted
        or faked it
          some twenty centuries ago
And they come to save him still
      in this sailless ark of a church
           adrift in the Mediterranean

#71

Shadows of seabirds
                    skim the waves
Halcyon
        makes its nest at sea
                floats where nothing floats
     except seaweed hair
                  of the seamen's goddess
        deep sea drowned

And I too have seen it

I too have heard it
              the voiceless keening
                  the sea's lips lapping
            off Carrara
                  or Andraitx Puerto
                  Majorca 1950
    where the dory listed leeward
                  and the flung net
                    fished the murex up
            drowned dark maiden
                  figlia di mare
            upon a shard
                  of Grecian urn
            (jettisoned in turn)

And none shall reach it now

                aie . . . aie . . .

                none shall hear it

                      the broken singing

72

The long boats

sail into the night—

Farewell!

#73

Somewhere on the coast of Greece

A bride in white
  A line of people in grey and black
        on one side of a broad grey river

A curtain of tall dark trees behind them

Beyond the trees a grey scrim of sky

Bride and groom are very far apart
He raises his arm as if to wave

It is late evening

The bride and the bridegroom kneel

The river
        hardly moving
                has the slow swell of an ocean

There is a slow music
                like the swell of an ocean

Love holds its breath

In the middle of the river
                in slow motion
                        a stork suspends its step

[90]

#74

Sewing two birds together
    since neither had sung a deep song
                in some time
Penelope thought the two white birds
                being birds of a feather
                    and sharing the same tongue
        might with one tongue create
                such a strange and beautiful melody
                that Ulysses still at sea
                        would hear it
            and the wind of their song
                    would carry him directly ashore
But the two birds
    needed more than one tongue
        to rejuvenate their art
        and to lure Ulysses
And the two tongue-tied birds
    in her tapestry
        could only sound a tragic droning
                reminiscent of some tyrant
                    talking though a mask
So when despairing late at night
    she unraveled her tapestry
        and freed their tongues
        the birds at once burst forth
                in free speech
And the rare song carried across the sea
                to the four round corners
                        of the flat earth
And the great sound reached Ulysses
            who then came cruising in

#75

The isles of Greece
        the isles of Greece
                upon a wine-dark sea
I started out once
        for an isle of Greece
                    in a Wanderjahr of wandering
And never thought that I might find it
                    only in myself
      A kind of island
             made of classic clarity
  where every work of art
              and every breathing thing
      is made of radiance

And there are tragic figures on it
                gesturing
But also
    lovely creatures on it still
                about to dance and sing

76

In the gardens of the Alhambra
                    I stole a small orange and ate it
The pulp dry and bitter
            and the juice
                    (acrid as an arab driven from his land)
                        made a desert of my mouth
                            and shriveled up my tongue
                                in the Sultan's last revenge
And I fell upon the ground
                  in a deep swoon
Deep as the *duende*
              in a gypsy's keening

77

They were shooting in the plazas

They were shooting in the *calles*

of Andalusia

They were shooting on the *playas*

They were shooting by the river

Where there was none like you Manina

Manina with your longing look

Your long yellow tresses Manina

Smelling of milk and chestnuts

Among the fireflies Manina

Among the mulberry trees

Parrots shriek in the patio

The cypress trees tremble

where they came for you Manina

They heard you singing then

when they shot you down Manina

And your last loud lament

Fell into Flamenco

#78

Took the seashore road
       and sat and watched the sea
A bird became a butterfly
        and landed on my knee
Who was the alien
     Whose land was it
         Whose sea?
She waved a wing tremulously
      not sure of anything
        the whole world swaying
And I
  not sure of anything
      agreed with everything
        that she was saying
As the pollen from her wings
      flowered down on me

#79

One great bird
        flew around silently
                high up
     under the panoply of trees
                  in the great rainforest
        under the great green trees
                at nightfall

He was no raven croaking 'Nevermore'
He was no falcon
        turning and turning
                in a widening gyre
He was no phoenix
        with wings afire
He was one huge
      still wild bird
  A flying mystery
        questioning me
             and our whole world
    flying silently
        from one roost to another
             high up in his wild rookery
     where all the birds were
          suddenly still
             suddenly motionless
Only he flew about
      noiselessly
His eye on this human
      in the wood of the world

80

And I sleeping dreamt
    of all the people of earth
                seen from a high helicopter
        And all of them as in a huge
                  round aquarium
      all swimming somewhere
            or on the bottom supine
     and others surfacing
          like dolphin leaping
            into the free air of our clime

And the dead
    the dead too were there

And did not rest

But traveled over the sea
        like gulls

81

Tonight at the great old beach hotel
under the swaying palms
the huge resort hostelry
on the white sand beach
with its elegant terraces and spouting fountains
and its stages with costumed native dancers
and its many elegant tables
with linen and silver and flickering candles
scattered on the terraces
around the oval illuminated swimming pool
with hanging lamps and candelabra
lighting white faces and bodies
flabby in flowered shirts and summer dresses
gold bracelets gleaming
and the indentured strolling mariachis
in silver-studded charros and huge sombreros
with marimbas and guitarras
and the hurrying dark waiters in white
and fireworks falling through the tropical sky
the soft air filled with soft laughter and tinkling glasses
the whole scene pulsing like a huge accordion
And I saw the whole sounding set
                fall into silence and darkness
            adobe arches and trellised terraces
                                    tumbled into ruin
        table-silver rusted away
                            by the pool cracked and dry
            full of broken alabaster statues
                                    dead iguanas and geckos
And myriad wooden coffins
                setting forth under sail

Over abandoned casinos
    pleasure domes and ragtime utopias
                          narco-corridas and stolen *ajidos*
All to the sound of the ocean's 'long withdrawing roar'

And I keeping watch from the far shore

82

The Spanish ants
         in their trance-dance
                     around the spilled honey
          in the Santa Barbara sun
Like last night
   at the Yoga Institute—
         Adepts at ecstasy
              blissed-out on tofu & bean sprouts
      trance-dancing to tantric mantras
             and the drum's wild honey
Not like now
     by the David Hockney swimming pool
              all blue and blue azure
       in the whirlpool bath
    two retired salesmen talking
    about turning yourself into
         'an industry-type guru' and
        'throwing your flesh against airplanes' and
       flying all over the country
            in alien space capsules
           at thirty-five thousand feet
      The airplane the ultimate loneliness
                Strangers six abreast
   To peddle pieces of paper
             with ciphers written on them
Between motel rooms without your wife
                  and nothing to do but drink
       and think of your own
            zero-sum life

83

A lion came to my window
                    and leaped in
As I ran out naked
          slamming the door of the cabin
                    and closing the window
     and looking in at the lion

He was trying on my hats
          and looking in the mirror
                 and browsing on my pot plant
After a while he lay down
          with his feet in the air
And I ran off into the world
      without the baggage of
               my clothes and my name
And soon developed
          a long tail
         a noble look
        and a mane
          and a taste for MGM movies

84

Summer passed me by

And every season
                    becomes the same season

Winter or summer passes by
                        in my high flat
No one notices the leaves
                coming and going
                        and falling
                            to the cry of flutes
The neighbor must
            cut down his tree
                    to save his sidewalk

The dog sleeps by the tv
                    unaware of Spring at the door
                        leaves in her hair
                        her breasts
                        flowered with petals

And an ancient voice in the air
                    singing *Primavera! Primavera!*

85

So much depends upon
                the very yellow taxicab
             at six
                   of a rainy morning
     lighting up a landscape
          from which we would elope
  as it appears
       at a distant intersection

  the very sum
       of human hope

86

The dog hangs his snout
                        out the auto window
Too long city-pent
                  his nose is out for wild game
His tongue hangs out
                   when he gets the scent
              of small creatures in the underbrush
         for whom every car is a brush
                         with disaster
And the dog feels for them
                   with his so sad eyes
        but looks at them
                  through the eyes of his master

#87

The tiny little ragged mutt
                in his little plaid jacket
        leads on a leash
                        his homeless mother
        clad in the same sad plaid
                        of a tattered blanket
        in which they'd been sleeping
                                before they were rousted

And the blind wind rises

And where will he lead her
                both dumb in their traces?

They still have each other

And still there is
                light if not hope
                                in their faces

88

I saw two lovers
                in a doorway in the rain
I saw a dog with three legs
                     with a bark and a bite
I saw a bird without a song
                in flight
I saw a drunk singing like a bird
I saw the Mountains of the Morn
                  sweep down to the sea
I saw nudes in art school
                drawing each other
I saw two lovers
           beating each other
I heard a field of crickets
                rubbing their legs together
                in ecstasy in summer
I saw the world turning
           under the sun
         when day was almost done
I saw the century
          stagger past in a dream
I saw time scroll on
           as we surfed through it
                morphing into eternity

89

I saw one of them sleeping
                huddled under cardboard
                              by the Church of Saint Francis
I saw one of them
                rousted by the priest

I saw one of them squatting in bushes

I saw another staggering
                against the plateglass window
                              of a firstclass restaurant

I saw one of them in a phone booth
                            shaking it
I saw one with burlap feet

I saw one in a grocery store
                    come out with a pint
I saw another come out
                with nothing
I saw another putting a rope
                  through the loops of his pants
I saw one
        with a bird on his shoulder
I saw one of them singing
                on the steps of City Hall
                        in the so cool city of love
I saw one of them trying to give
                    a lady cop a hug
I saw another sleeping
                by the Brooklyn Bridge
I saw another standing
                by the Golden Gate

The view from there was great

90

Passed the Bouncer's Bar tonight
in its old leaning building
just off the Embarcadero
Lots of stiffs in there
still nursing their beers
and staring at the wall
It was that kind of place
long on atmosphere
and short on talk
Even the bartender kept silent
having long ago given up bar banter
There was no Happy Hour in here
even in the bad old days
Nothing relieved the gloom
on days like this
The swinging door
rarely swung
The bums crept in out of the sun
Only the jukebox once in a while
showed signs of life
now and then letting out late at night
an old broken moan
about a dude leaving his wife
and how she done him wrong for a song
While an old head in a corner
mumbles and sings along
And falls out into the night
with its pathless starry sky
And raises a fist
to those black heavens
And lets out a bloody cry

91

The Green Street Mortuary Marching Band
        marches right down Green Street
              and turns into Columbus Avenue
             where all the café sitters at
                 the sidewalk café tables
                    sit talking and laughing and
                     looking right through it
   as if it happened every day in
    little old wooden North Beach San Francisco
    but at the same time feeling thrilled
        by the stirring sound of the gallant marching band
       as if it were celebrating life and
                 never heard of death

And right behind it comes the open hearse
    with the closed casket and the
        big framed picture under glass propped up
        showing the patriarch who
              has just croaked
And now all seven members of
    the Green Street Mortuary Marching Band
     with the faded gold braid on their
             beat-up captains' hats
        raise their bent axes and
        start blowing all more or less
             together and
   out comes this Onward Christian Soldiers like
       you heard it once upon a time only
           much slower with a dead beat

And now you see all the relatives behind the
       closed glass windows of the long black cars and

                    their faces are all shiny like they
                       been weeping with washcloths and
                          all super serious
                    like as if the bottom has just dropped out of
                       their private markets and
              there's the widow all in weeds, and the sister with the
bent frame and the mad brother who never got through school and
Uncle Louie with the wig and there they all are assembled together
and facing each other maybe for the first time in a long time but their
masks and public faces are all in place as they face outward behind
the traveling corpse up ahead and oompah oompah goes the band
very slow with the trombones and the tuba and the trumpets and the
big bass drum and the corpse hears nothing or everything and it's a
glorious autumn day in old North Beach if only he could have lived
to see it Only we wouldn't have had the band who half an hour later
can be seen straggling back silent along the sidewalks looking like
hungover brokendown Irish bartenders dying for a drink or a last
hurrah

92

How fragile the flesh
   how fragile the world around it
      this life on earth evanescent
               deep in samsara
How transient these
        solid ephemeral buildings
      Concrete bastions
           piled up brick & mortar
Wooden caravansaries
         built on sand
    Crystal cities alight
        Spectral skyscrapers
          sheathed in glass
          vaulted in night
    Houses of cards
       in sleeping suburbias
   Barrios of shacks
      made of mud and chewing gum
Fiberglass cars and transient trains
      (prairie schooners into Pullmans)
         sheeted in oblivion
    Transient their tracks and stations
        their 'salles des pas perdus'

How fragile the bodies pulsing in them
         (Each a temporary shell
          housing a life)
  Ballroom dancers (husband and wife)
    statuesque secretaries
      blondes in porn videos
        heavies in heroic operas
  Bodhisattvas bathing in Ganges—

How fragile this frieze of mummers
                    this dumb show—transubstantial pageant!
    Gone in a breath—

Pale idols in the night streets
                    dance and bound to death

93

The population explodes
        and the sun wears shades
              and clouds have trousers
And the Third World War
          will be the war against the Third World
As homeless hordes sweep the earth
       and the sun the sun
            is carried away in a cloud
And every ethnicity
       insists aloud
          on its own ethnicity
And the sun muddies and darkens
  and the old Man in the Moon
    being a negative of the sun
      hides his face in a cloud
          which carries him away
And the new Cold War
  is the war with the great god computer
    and its mantra is
      Jai Ram Jai Ram CD Rom CD Rom Jai Ram
As the whole world spins
       on internets or outernets
         in a huge mystic void
     a virtual vacuum in
      the huge picture-tube
         of the world
And its screen is swept
     with alarms and excursions
          struggle and flight
   where virtual armies clash by night

94

So show your son a sunset
                          before they're all gone
              advised an old Lefty
                          exhibiting the usual paranoia
                                            of the Left
              that has now spilled over
                          on ecologists
                          and others of their ilk
      always ranting about
              the ozone hole and
              cancer and smoking and
                          the population of the world
                                      doubling again
                          by the year two thousand twenty
      and about how the earth
                          is coming to a sudden
                                      bad end
Whereas we all know the media and
              the oil combines and
              the tobacco companies and
                          the industry scientists and
              the industrial perplex in general
                          are all telling us the whole bull
                                      and nothing but the bull
So no need to worry
                  'No problem'
                          as they say downtown
Even if those clouds out the window
                          look a bit strange
And the droughts all over the world
              aren't really all that bad
                  because it can't happen here
                          as they used to say in the Thirties

[114]

And all those jet-streams from airlines
                         really don't spew more
                                cancerous exhaust
                                       than a billion cars
And those aren't really
                         Sun Dogs in the too-brilliant sun
And sunsets are still sunsets
                    even if they are only
                                       one-color sunsets
       over which pilots are reporting
                    clouds are lower than they used to be
                                before the Greenhouse years
Whereas sunsets now are more like 'heart events'
       with pollution like bad cholesterol
              jamming the arteries of the universe
              and obstructing circulation
              and causing systemic disasters

And our evening spread across the sky
                         like a patient etherised upon a table

95

At night
      a dying star
            falls in a field afar
At dawn
      a bird
         perched above it
               sings an obit

96

Great river

      Image of time

And every evening

          radiant alphabets

                rise over it

In which I would decipher
             Your inscrutable name

97

But what is that laughter under the hill

It's the laughter of the Marvelous
                    of the Invisible
                            of the Absurd
Since there isn't any longer any Away
        (On the island furthest out
            there's a Club Med)
                        we seek the island inside us
                    an island in the sun
                        a wild calypso place
                            an isle of last escape
            the land that is unconquerable
                                that cannot be consumed
There is a passionate yearning
                a longing for wildness
                    a love of wildness
                            at the heart of every history
From Caliban to Gauguin
    from Rousseau's noble savage
        to Rimbaud's Drunken Boat
                and Whitman's first barbaric yawp
From the Roanoke colonists
                (who disappeared into the wilderness
                    leaving a note behind:
                            'Gone to Croatoan')
        to London's Call of the Wild
            to Kerouac's Cassady
                    whose hotrod was his horse
        and Ken Kesey in his bus
            with sign reading "Further"
                            on the last frontier

It is land of heretics and witches
   runaway slaves and mountainmen
      Burning Men and *poètes maudits*

We hear their high laughter
   We hear their high keening
        here at the end of the world

#98

Suddenly

in the long door of night

Fireflies

99

At the Golden Gate

A single plover far at sea
        wings across the horizon

A single rower almost out of sight
                rows his skull
                      into eternity

And I take a buddha crystal in my hand
            And begin becoming pure light

100

And are we not then in the real Paradiso not in Dante's old holy
heaven as painted by Gustav Doré whose clouds were angels but
here at this seaside Sun Festival on this far Western shore on this
new world border on this glorious Sunday morning and people grow-
ing more beautiful all the time with the rising sun painting their
upturned faces as if all time were standing still and all would live
forever and limbs and faces never wither in this moment dancing like
sibyls with the Golden Bough upraised against the sky and girls in
long white dresses dancing in the surf to the sound of flutes and
bongos as if this were the hippie Sixties once again but it isn't it's the
visionary end of our flaming century here on this far beach and
children with garlands leading ponies with flowers in their bridles
and barking dogs behind them and other wet mutts bringing sticks
and mothers in madras dresses bringing newborn babes to be bap-
tized by a very tall young long-haired shaman in feathered cape who
holds high each babe in turn and facing the sun proclaims it blessed
by great god sun and proclaims the shining name of this new arrival
on earth and proclaims its true age on earth 'Twenty days!' 'Six
days!' 'Three weeks!' and all will live forever and forever and
forever in this shining moment in our own immortal time

101

Wearing Apollinaire's derby I am in a zeppelin with a hundred
dignitaries in tailcoats from all over the world cruising about looking
for a place to declare peace personal and universal Looking for a soft
landing for peace on earth Gardens are sighted on the horizon and
the airship veers in that direction only to discover there is no airfield
and we veer off again The sky is lit with flares A man in tails with
wings jumps off the Eiffel Tower thinking he's a bird He plummets
straight down in front of his friends I am a boy picking petals off a
sunflower in Provence It's midsummer A million crickets sound
their huge drone in the night A sunflower leans in a window where I
am a boy leaning out *Loulou Loulou* someone calls I have picked all
the petals They fall *Loulou Loulou où est tu* It is hot in the dark room
There are riots in France and Italy *The Americans killed Sacco and
Vanzetti* I saw Lindbergh land The zeppelin sails on There is jazz on
the wireless It's Sidney Bechet Paris 1930s the dignitaries toasting
each other in champagne and American cigarettes The pilot sends a
Morse code greeting to a ship at sea The band plays on The Captain
sends back a round of drinks on the house sailing through the hot
night an endless flight around the world We gaze out the portals of
the crystal gondola at the endless stars Night reveals the cities of
earth lit with leftover sun I am kneeling in short pants in a cathedral
somewhere in France Christ died on Friday and rose on Sunday
setting a world altitude record out of sight in an instant in the dark
firmament I don't believe a word of it The wine doesn't taste like
blood The dirigible soars in the summit of heaven Where will it ever
land The eternal pilot pours over the charts The dawn is pointing On
a lake far below the wood boats knock together Life sails on I am
stretched out in a sailing-canoe in upstate New York An eagle soars
in the summit of heaven An opera hat lies on a marble table in the
lobby of the Paris opera High over the city a plane searches the sky
making a sound like a gnat It's a plane it's a bird There is a thrill in
the air We are walking down the Avenue de l'Opéra The Metro
entrance yawns with its Art Nouveau mouth and swallows us The
zeppelin flies on into the twenty-first century The zeppelin is life

itself The zone we fly through endless without borders without boundaries There are no more nations Migrant populations sweep the earth in search of food and shelter We throw down our champagne glasses The tv shows the endless night sky We are watching an eclipse The universe endless stretches away in endless night There must be a place where all is light Where then O Endless One in endless eternity Where now We are heavenly bodies rapt in time hurtling through bent space Flame-outs illuminate the landscape

INDEX OF
FIRST LINES

INDEX OF FIRST LINES